Floodgate Poetry Series
Volume 7

March 2022

Chris + Tae,

It was so good to see y'all + to finally get to hang out with Elliott! Hope to spend time again together before much time passes.

Much love,
D

Etchings Press
Indianapolis, Indiana

Floodgate Poetry Series
Volume 7

Barbara Robidoux
Donovan McAbee
Kimiko Hahn

Series edited by
Andrew McFadyen-Ketchum

This publication is made possible by funding provided by the Shaheen College of Arts and Sciences and the Department of English at the University of Indianapolis.

UNIVERSITY *of*
INDIANAPOLIS.

Published by Etchings Press
University of Indianapolis
1400 E. Hanna Ave.
Indianapolis, IN 46227

etchings.uindy.edu
www.uindy.edu/cas/english

Printed by IngramSpark

Published in the United States of America

ISBN 978-0-9988976-5-3

The book interior is set with the Charter family. The cover is set in Franklin Gothic Book and Charter.

Cover image by Brenda Butka
Cover and interior design by Hope Coleman
Donovan McAbee photo by Miriam Berkley

Contents

STIRRING SORROW INTO SOUP

Barbara Robidoux

Sightings

Donovan McAbee

wind chime, whale, and downpour
Kimiko Hahn

STIRRING SORROW
INTO SOUP

Barbara Robidoux

This book is dedicated
to the breath of the desert,
this dry land that continues to be
reborn.

Most of these short poems were written in the months preceding a planetary pandemic which descended on this earth. Some of the prose pieces (Haibun) rose out of the plague time itself in a new reality of sheltering in place and social distancing. We are in the midst of a transitional time for all humans and the planet herself. Our future is mostly uncertain. I hope these short poems can offer some solace.

—On a windy spring day, Santa Fe, New Mexico 2020

HAIKU

SHE KEEPS A DUSTPAN
ON A WINDOWSILL
TO CATCH THE STAR DUST

COLD SPRING MORNING
THE MATING SAGE GROUSE
DRINKS RAIN

EARLY SPRING
SANDHILL CRANES MIGRATE NORTH
THEIR ANCIENT GURGLINGS

MARCH WINDS
PUSH HARD AGAINST WINTER
A LONE DAFFODIL HOLDS TIGHT

IN THE DOORYARD
HONEYSUCKLE MAKES BUDS
IGNORES WINTER SNOW

SPRING BLIZZARDS
PEACH BLOSSOMS RELUCTANT
TO SHOW THEIR GLORY

MORNING AFTER
APRIL SNOWS
LIMP LILACS

APRICOTS IN FULL BLOOM
ALONG AGUA FRIA ROAD
FAINT SCENT OF SKUNK

AT ATACAMA DESERT
AFTER YEARS WITHOUT RAIN
GLOBE MALLOWS CARPET THE EARTH

LENTICULAR CLOUDS
LOOM OVER THE DESERT
SCENT OF CHAPARRAL

PLANTING BUDDLEIA
TO CALL BUTTERFLIES
RABBITS RESPOND

RAIN CLOUDS
OVER THE BARRANCAS
THE LEOPARD FROG SINGS

LOVE UNSPOKEN LEARNED FROM
THE QUIVER OF APPLE BLOSSOMS
WHILE THUNDER CRASHES

MORNING I TOUCH YOU
LIKE SPRING SNOW TOUCHES BARE SKIN
AND DISSOLVES

I COMB TANGLES
FROM MY LONG HAIR
LEARN FREEDOM'S LONELINESS

PEACH BLOSSOMS FROZEN
BY COLD AND LATE SNOW
THE ACHE OF SPRINGTIME

AT CABALLO LAKE
A FIREBALL LIGHTS THE SKY
YOUR GREEN EYES

AT THE STATION
THE TRAIN PULLS SLOWLY AWAY
ONE HAND WAVING FROM A WINDOW

OUT OF ROCKS
PAINTED WITH STORIES
STAR PEOPLE WALKED INTO MY LIFE

EMPTY WOODEN BOAT
IS TAKEN BY THE TIDE
FOOTPRINTS IN THE SAND

FAR FROM THE SEA
THE TIDE STILL RUNS IN MY BLOOD
SHIPWRECKED IN THE HIGH DESERT

TURQUOISE CLOUDS
OF MOUNTAIN BLUEJAYS
OVER A HIDDEN POND

AT THE BOSQUE
ONE ASIAN CRANE
AMIDST A THOUSAND SANDHILLS

A NOVEL VIRUS SPREADS
OVER THE PLANET
ONE WORLD ENDS, ANOTHER BEGINS

EVEN AS MILLIONS DIE
APRICOTS BLOOM
THIS PANDEMIC SPRING

A PATCH OF PURPLE IRIS
BLOOMS, THEN BLOOMS AGAIN
CORONA VIRUS SCREAMS

UNDER A FULL MOON
BIRCHES BENT WITH SNOW
SHE STIRS SORROW INTO THE SOUP

TANKA

GENERATIONS
STUMBLE TO EL NORTE
ON THEIR PATH
ONE HUNDRED YEAR OLD SAGUAROS
HEAVE GREAT SIGHS

BROWNSVILLE TEXAS
BURY MY HEART AT WALMART
NO PLAY DOUGH HERE
ONLY STOLEN CHILDREN
ASSIGNED NUMBERS, NO NAMES

MY COUNTRY CAGES CHILDREN
A CASH CROP
IN PRIVATE PRISONS
STOLEN FROM THEIR FAMILIES
WHILE A PANDEMIC RAGES

IN THE DESERT
BARREL CACTUS
ALWAYS LEAN SOUTH
COMPASSES FOR ILLEGALS
WALKING TO EL NORTE

HUNDREDS OF GEMINIDS
PER HOUR
THOUSANDS OF MIGRANTS
SEEK ASYLUM
MY SILENCE SEVERED

GRANDMOTHER HAD NO PAPERS
MOTHER HAS NO PAPERS
THIS CHILD IS PAPERED
SNOW SLAMS AGAINST MY FACE
IN THIS NORTHERN CITY

THE DEAD DISSOLVE
INTO THE MISTS
BONES UPON BONES LEFT
IN THIS CHANGING LIGHT
OF FALL INTO WINTER

A MASKED MOTHER
MASKS HER CHILDREN
IMMIGRANTS, THEY SEEK
ASYLUM IN EL NORTE
PANDEMIC KNOWS NO BORDERS

YOU CALL ME
FROM THE FUNERAL HOME
YOUR GRANDDAUGHTER IS DEAD
RAIN NOT SEEN IN TWENTY YEARS
RUNS THE RIVER

AS GREENLAND MELTS
OCEANS RAGE AND RISE
YOU WAKE TO FIND
YOUR BACKYARD PICNIC TABLE
FLOATING IN THE BAY

AT THE BOTTOM
OF A ONCE INLAND SEA
BEAVERS BUILD THEIR HOMES
READ MESSAGES LEFT BY MY BREATH
IN THIS SMALL WILD PLACE

OUTSIDE THE WINDOW
WHITE BIRCHES BENT FROM SNOW
THE OLD WOMAN, ALSO BENT
STIRS HER SORROW
INTO WINTER SOUP

HAIBUN

MEMORY

I lay down in tall grasses flattened by beavers who came ashore to gather saplings for their home. They rested here and now I rest and watch the meandering Rio Chama make its way to the Rio Grande.

The river knows me by my breath. It slows and settles me into sleep. Water dreams.

I wake, step over a barbed wire fence, push aside river willows and cattails until I reach the shore. I bend to touch the water, it has lost its chill this autumn day. Overhead a great blue heron flies to the other side of the beaver dam and stops to fish.

The elders say the land and waters remember us. We leave our breath and our sweat wherever we walk. Memory lives in the place.

ancient cottonwoods

and the black bear

remember your laughter

SHELTER IN PLACE

Water flows from snowmelt in the mountains into the Santa Fe River. Purple and yellow wild mustard blooms all over town and wild iris open above Holy Ghost Canyon. In this high desert, curved bill thrashers make their nests in the arms of cane chollas and wait for magenta flowers to welcome their young.

And a virus spreads over the land. One American dies every 45 seconds, the living are told to "shelter in place."

As humans fall, the planet appears to heal. A pale green light spreads over the earth and plants awaken. We can breathe again. Without contrails the bluest desert skies turn even bluer.

a novel virus

circles the earth

red tailed hawks fly closer to home

EASTER SUNDAY 2020

300 million monarch butterflies are headed to New Mexico on their migration north. We will welcome them after months of sickness and grieving from the novel Covid-19 virus.

After a few weeks of above normal temperatures and spring weather, it comes on cold again with snow in Santa Fe. I cover snow peas and radishes with an old tablecloth and pick a bouquet of purple irises to bring inside.

The peach tree is flowering and setting fruit, apples and plums are slower, more cautious of the cold. I hold off installing a nucleus of honeybees. It is way too cold to open the hives. We all trust warmer weather will return.

When the pandemic ends it'll be all new, the old will die with the virus. Some say a portal will open, a gateway to a new world just big enough to walk through, our old baggage left behind.

purple irises shiver

in April's last snow

corona virus rages

DRAGONFLIES MIGRATE SOUTH

Overhead the gurgle of sandhill cranes announce their return to winter in our bosques. It is a gray day, snow is forecasted, welcome moisture for this dry land.

Violence and mass murders precede winter. Eleven Jews are slayed while praying in a Pittsburgh synogogue. Pipe bombs are sent to many others. At the same time Central Americans flee their homelands and walk the 2,000 miles to the United States southern border. They plea for entry and are refused. U.S. troops are sent to the border and are followed by a "civilian militia" manned by right wing racists filled with hatred. "If they throw rocks at you," the Trump president orders, "shoot them."

A cold rain pours down and I grieve under a slow turning moon. Winter moves in with snow sleet and tears. The sandhills return to our bosques and find solace without papers while dragonflies ignore borders and fly south.

a waning gibbous moon

watches without mercy

while dragonflies migrate south

THE THRASHER'S SONG

I have faith in seeds. They swell, crack open, sprout, flower and fruit. In the garden I make short rows with a long handled hoe. I stoop and place bean seeds in the furrows, then cover them with the red earth in my hands. In the high desert this is an act of love, of hope in a time of planetary pandemic.

I wonder about the grief American Chestnut trees felt when they were hit with plague. In the early 1900s nearly four billion trees died due to a fungus imported from Asia. The trees disappeared but somehow today they are still flowering on a downtown street.

More than 60 million Americans have already died from the Covid-19 virus in just four months. This is more than the number killed in the Vietnam war which lasted nineteen years. This is a timeless time. Day folds into day, week into week, month into month as we wait for a vaccine to save lives and suffering.

A pair of curved bill thrashers, immune to my fear and confusion, build a nest in the arms of a cane cholla growing by the beehives. Their love songs fill the air.

a respite from

fear and sadness

thrashers sing their love

DIA de los MUERTOS

Horses run free in the pueblo. Some drink from acequias. They are hungry horses. Along a chain link fence that borders the railroad tracks running through the pueblo someone has strung razor wire. After several deaths on the tracks nobody climbs the fence anymore. Four times a day the AMTRAK train shoots through the village. Behind a trailer a young man hangs played out parts of electric guitars on the fence. "They should know a musician lives here," he tells his sister.

Before dawn the sky filled with meteors. Orionids. Dust specks released from Haley's comet. Scientist say 62,000 fall per hour.

The calendario turns. Las Calaveras ride highway 285/84. Their carros speed through Chimayo, climb the road to Truchas. Snow does not slow them. They ride to cemetarios in the sky.

I bake pan de muerto. Raise my sumador to the west. Feed copal to the fire. Then scatter orange marigold petals by my door. Los Muertos will smell them and come in to visit.

life is a dream

full of tears

to die is to waken

STIRRING SORROW INTO SOUP

Warm winters were unknown until the climate changed. Even though the temperatures warmed, snow still came on heavy and lasted longer.

Trees questioned among themselves the changes. Birches bent lower and lower and broke with the weight of the heavy snow. Pines stood tall but refused to grow taller.

An old woman cooks a soup: potatoes, carrots, turnips and a bit of venison cut from the loin. On the cookstove she adds thyme, sage and salt from the sea.

She lets it simmer for hours then stirs the soup with a large wooden spoon that belonged to her mother. This spoon has stirred many soups, she thinks, *but none with the sorrow I feel today.*

a woodstove warms

a winter soup

snow slams against the window

Sightings

Donovan McAbee

Sightings

Shortly after her death, Mother Teresa appeared
in a cinnamon bun in Nashville, Tennessee.
She looked serious, perturbed even, as though
this epiphany were an inconvenience.

Once, in the nineties, when statues of the Virgin
were crying all over Ireland, one in Donegal
did not get the memo. A sign hung around
its neck announcing: THIS HOLY MOTHER OUT OF ORDER.

I found myself, two years after Mom died,
in the second pew from the front in a dark,
empty chapel. I looked up at the six-foot-tall
wooden Jesus, votive candles at his feet,

and I could see a tear falling over and over
down his right cheek, a trick of light and
shadow—but somehow, in that moment,
I knew they were for me, those tears.

On the Way to Church

Fast Fare, Sunday morning, Mama behind the wheel,
we fall out of our baby-blue four-door Ford
headed for aisles and aisles of almost-pure sugar:
gummy bears and worms, candy cigarettes
white with red tips like the real ones lit.
My hands full of treasure, a young Israelite
on the big trip out of Egypt, I size up
my brothers' shares—the youngest always
has the keenest sense of justice. In her dark-green
dress with eggshell white dots and shoes
that don't quite match it, Mama tells us
to bring our stuff to the counter, where her can of
Diet Coke sits, waiting for us like the church
we're headed to out in the country.

Mama's Economy

A bit of milk with the eggs
makes them go farther.

She kneads the dough,
rolls it out on the wax paper,
sprinkles a touch more flour.

She uses the biscuit-cutter
that belonged to her grandmother,
though she tells me,

the top of a drinking glass
works just the same.

Coming Back Down

What was it landed me
flat on my back against the floor
of that storefront church?

The preacher speaking in tongues
over my laid-out body as that
lonesome gospel lifted me elsewhere.

Mama helped me stagger to the car
once the service had ended.
I'd never been to a church like that.

I don't know what it was
made the preacher single me out.
Maybe I looked an easy target,

or maybe he read on my face the signs
of someone in need of a good dose of wonder.
Whatever it was, that afternoon

as we drove through the mountains,
I couldn't stop crying for the beauty of it all.

Mama's Body

The nurses remove the IV, take the tube
from your nose, move the bed to the center
of the room, so we can circle and pray.

Your spirit, because I believe on this day
in such a thing, has abandoned its husk,
lifted from the room, or walked out the door.

The marriage of body and breath broken—
Mama   not-Mama   Mama   my first home.

ii. *1960*

You woke to the sound of a vase
toppling off an end table—ran
from your bedroom down the hallway
to the door of the living room, where
your Mama lay on the floor, your Daddy
standing above her, calling her names
you were told not to repeat. You ran
back to your room, like you always did.

Years later, you tell me how you'd cover
your body in the sheets, pull the blanket
over your head, close your eyes
and pray to disappear, that the mattress
might swallow you like the ocean.

iii. *1966*

Some things better left unsaid,
so you thought for two-and-a-half
decades, while those secrets nursed dreams
that crawled through your nights—

how, after supper, your friend's Dad
would play strip poker with you
and her at the dining room table
when you were eleven, how he'd
take you later from the bed
where you slept, your friend's Mom

always in the kitchen washing up.

iv. *1977*

You at twenty-two sit on the couch,
rubbing your belly. You hold the
little yellow dress with white frills
that Grandma gave you.

At twenty weeks, the ultrasound's
silent scan. Daddy takes you
to the hospital, where the doctor
delivers the stillborn and carries it away.

Two years later, you put the yellow dress
on me, so you could imagine how beautiful
your little girl might have been.

v. 1985

I nuzzle into you on the couch,
rest in the crook your legs make
as you lie on your side. You stroke
my curly hair, and I go to sleep,
while you and Daddy watch TV.

You carry me then, down the hallway
to my bedroom, sing an ocean lullaby,
tuck me in snug-as-a-bug for the night.

vi. *1993*

You reach out for me, while we drive down 26,
put your hand on my knee, like you've always done—

I draw back, refuse the touch. You reach out
with your words to ask about my week, to find out

if there's some girl who's caught my eye. You make
this 350-mile round trip twice every other weekend—

more often when I ask you to, just to see me.

After the divorce, I fortify myself, won't let you

touch me. Won't let Dad touch me.

Don't want to let anyone touch me ever again.

vii. *2001*

Your arm bandaged to keep edema
from settling in. You retch into the plastic
pail the nurse gave you, a reaction
to the anesthesia. You apologize again,
for the inconvenience this has caused me,
as I look at the wound under your arm,
where the surgeon removed the lymph nodes.
I take you, next morning, back to the house
to wait for pathology to give us the verdict,
not breast cancer, as everyone has told us,
but melanoma—that word (melanoma) we hear
(melanoma) spread through (melanoma) every
word (melanoma) we speak (melanoma) those
three (melanoma) last (melanoma) years.

viii. *date uncertain*

there must have
been moments
when it felt
like yours

when it didn't belong
to fear or pain
or to a man
or a child

times when your
long dark hair
brushed your shoulders
on a windy day

when the sun
warmed your skin
and you felt the glory
of this other belonging

Grief

I've woken in strange places—
facedown on church pews and sidewalks,
covered with dew in the grass
of the graveyard; considered how
the ocean washes the rocks
below the cliff under moonlight.

Those last memories still wound:
the uncomfortable recliner
I made a bed of in the hospital room,
rubbing lotion on your swollen feet,
whispering what I hoped you could hear—
I love you and *It's okay when you need to leave.*

Hamstrung

Why don't you shovel away
the slagheap at my window?
I'm busy pulling weeds in the garden.

I caught a parable and threw it back.
Like hay in a needle-stack
I've kept my ointment in a jar of flies.

Swallowing the Camel

My faith is a gnat,
my devotion a polished
stone, my fears
a dog whimpering.
When I was a kid,
Jesus talked to me
just for the asking,
the son of God
squeezed me in, made
time in the evenings
for all that twilight angst.

Tonight, there's silence
and its echo.
There's waiting,
like the feeling you get
in the family room
at the hospital when
someone you love
goes under the knife.

Outside the Mediation

Had I snuck up and yelled *surprise,*
or grabbed him from behind,
I have no doubt his heart would have
convulsed inside his chest. Had I tapped
the bottom of his cane with the force
of a dog's breath, I am certain he would have
stumbled to the concrete floor. As the sedan
pulled around the corner of the garage
and came to a stop, his wife got out
of the driver's side, her face flushed of color.
She thought she knew what I was thinking,
that I could just as well see him buried
as standing there, arrogant as he had been,
thinking by the sight of that mole
he could tell with his own two eyes
if it were melanoma, that tiny black spot
behind Mama's ribcage numbed,
he made his incision and stitched it shut.
How strange it all seemed to me as well,
he and I making small talk about the weather,
their grandkids at college, and the drive home
they'd make down Interstate 20.

Sunday Lunch from Geri's Restaurant

Easy on the curves so the gravy
doesn't make the bread soggy
in the Styrofoam boxes. Slow
by our old brick church house
where Pentecostal Ukrainians
worship now. In the cemetery
out back Grandpa and Grandma
McAbee laid out together
underneath the ground across from
the Culbreth farm. That's the curve
I wrecked Daddy's truck on—
skidded on an ice-patch left
under pine-tree shade a full week
after all the snow was gone.
My buddy's eyes got bigger
than his head as we spun and spun
almost forever in the Sunday-night
darkness. Sweet tea's on the counter
when I get home. Daddy and I
open our boxes as though they're
Christmas presents, happy that
by some stroke of fortune
we got just what we asked for.

The two-foot-tall devil that lives in my cupboard

I can't imagine what he wants here,
spending all this time on me. Certainly,
when it comes to the scalping of souls,

there can't be such a high price on my head.
After all, I'm just a regular Joe,
pants-on-one-leg-at-a-time kind of guy.

I hardly believe in God anymore, much less
the little creatures on the other side.
Maybe he's a memory that refuses to leave, the shadow

of a ghost buried deep, but I swear those are his paw prints
across the kitchen floor, the ones I get down
on my hands and knees each night to scrub away.

Anecdotal Evidence for the Existence of God

Orgasms
Cotton candy
Chocolate covered almonds
Coffee

River stones

That time after praying when I would have doubted
my own existence before I would have doubted
God's

Tortoises
Ice cream
The ocean

Anecdotal Evidence against the Existence of God

The poor design and frequent malfunctioning of the
prostate gland

Licorice
World War II
Dysentery

The Godfather: Part III

All those times after praying when I went away
empty

Mosquitoes
Standardized tests
Every square inch of Orlando, Florida

Field Research

"I am not an ornithologist—I am a bird" —Saul Bellow

A tree is not an arborist,
   nor a bird an ornithologist,
      nor, for that matter, God a theologian.

But we are all anthropologists,
   all arborists, ornithologists,
      all theologians, no matter how poorly trained.

Observe me, for instance,
   I couldn't tell a birch from a sugar maple
      if a white-billed woodpecker's life depended on it.

And God, that cuckoo bird, whose call I've heard,
   makes its nest in a tree I have no name for
      in a forest I cannot seem to find.

As We Enter Heaven

Not beyond the threshold of all imagining,
or on the other side of those gates
white as a movie star's teeth in that city
with gleaming streets, but here in this small town
of desire, where the movie poster is peeling off,
the five and dime shuttered, where teenage boys
smoke cigarettes and look at dirty magazines
in the park. Bless us here, Father, in this
breathing moment. Bless us here, as we enter
heaven, one dying prayer at a time.

Instructions for Prayer

Tear yourself away from the illusion
that anyone owes you anything,
especially that friend you lent fifty bucks to.
Consider it a gift, like light like breath.

Tear yourself away from the illusion
that the things you cling to will cling to you
when your grip loosens and your fingers slip;
it's easier letting go before you have to.

And while you're at it, this task of
slaughtering sacred cows, go ahead and
tear yourself away from the illusion
that the earth will miss your footsteps,

the air your breath, and that anyone's life,
besides your own, can't go on without you.

Holy the Body

I've thought so little of you that now
you seek your revenge in the grinding
of kneecaps, the tightening of hamstrings,
loss of elasticity, the skin. So long neglected,
you weren't even an afterthought. I apologize
each morning with a handful of pills. Oh,
scarred flesh of me in the mirror, as I turn the page
on another decade, I bless the stretch marks
on my stomach, evidence of those dead years
when food was my one friend. I bless
the crow's feet at the corners of my eyes,
proof of days spent under the sun. I bless the gray
in my beard, reminder that sometimes,
despite ourselves, wisdom appears.
I bless our breaking down, dear body,
pray the process is slow, that when time
confronts us with its choices, you'll teach me
when to hold on, when to let go.

After the Fact

I know you by the space
you leave empty.

I draw lines in the air
where the roof used to be.

I wait for you, Lord,
like a mailbox for a letter.

The grass still wonders
how the ground got there.

wind chime, whale,
and downpour

Kimiko Hahn

for my students
A B a A a b A B

Good Housekeeping, 1960

Mother knelt in the weeds
yanking tenderly so as to get the tendrils.
In *Good Housekeeping* she'd read up
on how to really get into the weeds
whether a garden or an infant's needs
or paying off that figurative bill.
Mother knelt in beds of weeds
intent on yanking every last tendril.

To save the cellphone battery—

I look up and through the train window.
There are stops I've not seen
since childhood—Spuyten Duyvil, Ludlow.
I look through the train window now
at trees in vacant lots that will grow
anywhere because they're not trees.
I keep looking out the window
because stopping cannot be seen.

Seeing Someone Seeing

Someone with a cellphone camera
noticed a whale in the Buttermilk Channel
and clicked a shot of its aura,
just a random someone with a camera.
How often do we see phenomena—
a robin or turtle hatching? Or an angel
of a child with a camera
capturing her whale in the Buttermilk Channel?

Private Coordinates

Where were you when the whale,
a blue one, swept under your ship
then rose up in its own wave gale?
Where were you when the whale
I thought I was struck its tail
starboard to storm and tilt
where you were when the whale,
a blue one, wept under your ship—?

For Eunice in Gambier

Eunice, I envy you your hummingbird,
and you, my firefly!
Without either, we'd feel bored!
Eunice, yes, I envy your hummingbirds—
Envy, a rapture-filled abode:
one hums, one fires (both eventual pyre).
Eunice, you envy my hummings and birds!
And I, your fires that fly!

The Toddler's Lexicon

She tells me *belly button*
and points to my navel.
I tell her, *it's 'oheso' in Japan*
and she repeats *belly button*.
I want to bestow alien diction,
as nothing less than marvel.
She points to her belly button,
Grandma, here's my jewel.

Riotous Dysnomia

She mistakes one word for another—
something her brain naturally concocts.
Her unruly gray matter and her heart
mistake one word for another
—*cleaver* for *leaver, cistern* for *sister*—
even *members* for *cocks*.
She mistakes one word for a mother—
something her brain preternaturally rocks.

The Dream Act

The border comes and goes
for hands and feet and words.
No matter city, personality, or rose
the border comes and goes.
Yes, from crown to toes
for coyote as well as bird.
But the border never goes
for this child's dream foreword.

Fall Equinox for Meena

As the decades arrive and fall off,
the day we met enjoys the fragrance of legend:
yes, we were crossing Amsterdam at 110th.
As the decades arrive and fall off,
we read to one another over spirits—
drafts about continents and husbands.
As the decades arrived and fell off,
our meeting glows with the fragrance of legend.

Competing Interests

Living in the country is living with quiet
except for the neighbor's competing roosters
keeping awake the couple and their infant
after moving to the country to live in quiet.
The wife purchased a white-noise gadget,
one with wind chime, whale, and downpour
just to live in a countrified quiet
complete with exceptional roosters.

My Little Translation

The Italians have an unforgettable phrase,
diritto all'oblio, the right to be forgotten,
though Mother didn't teach me this in my nursery.
My Italian has unforgettable phrases,
most having to do with *cioccolato al latte*—
my pinafore—and *pasticchiona girl* in Rome.
That unforgettable Italian phrase
I revised to *the rite to be forgotten.*